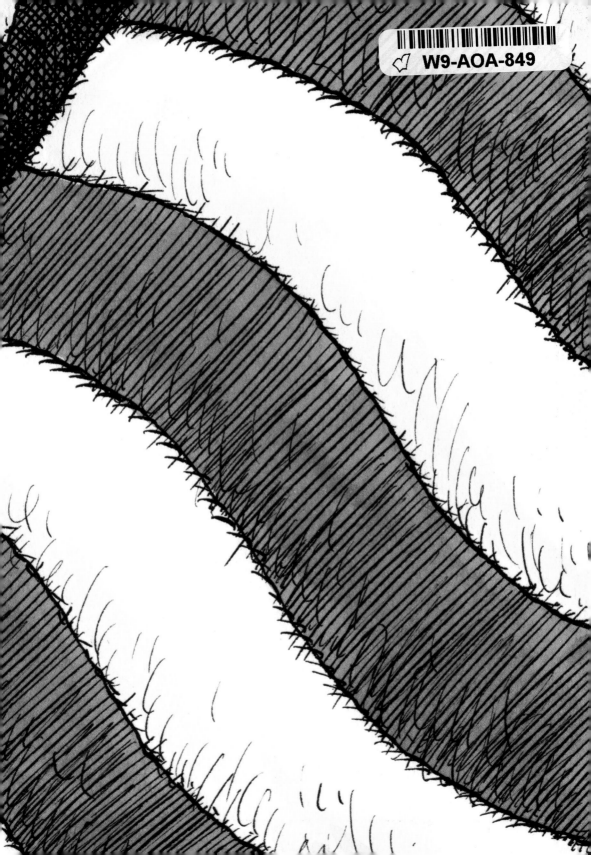

W9-AOA-849

TO ALL WHO

LOVE FREEDOM —

IN AMERICA AND

AROUND THE WORLD!

— EM & TR

Text Copyright © 2019 by Metaxas Media, LLC
Illustrations Copyright © 2019 by Tim Raglin

All rights reserved. No part of this publication may be reproduced or transmitted in any form or by any means electronic or mechanical, including photocopy, recording, or any information storage and retrieval system now known or to be invented, without permission in writing from the publisher, except by a reviewer who wishes to quote brief passages in connection with a review written for inclusion in a magazine, newspaper, website, or broadcast.

Regnery® is a registered trademark of Salem Communications Holding Corporation

Cataloging-in-Publication data on file with the Library of Congress

ISBN: 978-1-68451-029-0
Ebook ISBN: 978-1-68451-032-0

Published in the United States by
Regnery Publishing
A Division of Salem Media Group
300 New Jersey Ave NW
Washington, DC 20001
www.Regnery.com

Manufactured in the United States of America

2019 Printing

Books are available in quantity for promotional or premium use. For information on discounts and terms, please visit our website: www.Regnery.com

DONALD
BUILDS THE WALL!

BY
ERiC METAXAS
& TiM RAGLIN

REGNERY
PUBLISHING
A Division of Salem Media Group

Once upon a time, long, long ago,

all the people lived in caves.

But the cave people were very happy.

A caveman named Donald once drained

the smelly money swamp that had

surrounded them.

Their old king and all his nasty

Swamp Creatures had run away.

Now the cave people were free!

They made Donald their president.

A president is a leader who helps his people.

Donald and all the cave people helped each other,

and together they made their country great again!

Everything became more and more wonderful!

They named their new country "The Land of the Free."

And the people were known as the Free People.

Word soon spread of the Land of the Free!

There were many swampy lands with kings and queens

who paid no attention to the people they ruled over.

So when those people heard about a place

where you could be free and govern yourself,

they couldn't get there fast enough!

They came in droves and contributed to

the wonderful society being created.

One man was an inventor who rubbed two sticks together.

He invented fire!

Because of it, everyone was able to cook their food!

And stay warm when it got cold.

Another man invented something he called a wheel!

But it was square and didn't work well.

Then another man invented one that was round.

This worked much better.

The Free People called this "competition in the free market."

It made everyone more prosperous than ever!

Things were so terrific that more and more people came,

all contributing something different to the wonderful Land of the Free.

But a few bad apples snuck in too.

They didn't abide by the laws of the Free People

and were generally nothing but trouble.

Some broke things and some even stole!

The WORST was a vicious gang called MSNBC–13!

When the Free People realized what was happening,

they told these troublemakers that freedom was a privilege

—that came with great responsibilities.

Then they escorted them to the border and told them that until

they were interested in taking freedom seriously,

they had to go back to their own land and be ruled by a king.

But weeks later, some of them snuck back in!

So Donald gathered everyone to talk about this problem.

How could they let in those who loved freedom

—but keep out those who didn't?

Donald had an idea!

"We could build a wall!" he said.

"They work very, very well. Really terrific."

"You're right!" someone said. "We didn't have a wall

at the front of our cave,

and bad people came in and stole things!

So we built a wall with a door, and the problem was solved."

"The wall we build will be big and beautiful!" Donald said.

"And it will have a big, beautiful door—

so that we can let anyone in who loves freedom!"

All the people cheered.

And so, working together, they started building the wall.

And it WAS big and beautiful, with a door to match.

But far, far away, the Swamp Creatures

were having a different problem.

They had chased the dirty swamp money all the way

to the horizon.

They settled right where the money piled up.

And every day they did the only thing they knew how to do:

They spent it.

And pretty soon the huge pile had disappeared.

"Back in the swamp, there was always plenty of money!

But where did it come from?"

"From the people outside the swamp," said the Lobby-o-saurus,

"they earned it by working."

"Working!? Ugh! You don't expect us to work!

Work is for those who are uncultured!"

"—And uneducated!"

"—And don't forget deplorable!"

"We—on the other hand—

are made for spending!"

"RIGHT! BUT FIRST WE NEED OTHER PEOPLE'S MONEY!" roared the George-o-saurus.

While the Swamp Creatures were talking,

the trees filled with bluebirds.

They had just come from the Land of the Free.

They kept tweeting about all the great things in

the cave people's new country.

"The people are doing

better than ever!"

"Things are so great that people are coming

from miles and miles away!"

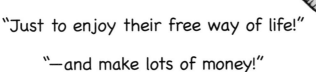

"Just to enjoy their free way of life!"

"—and make lots of money!"

The Swamp Creatures got really mad when they heard this.

"It's NOT FAIR the cavemen have so much good stuff!"

"It's because they've stolen what was ours!

That was OUR land!

So whatever they've got there is ours too!"

"We've got to go back there

and demand our fair share of what they've got!"

So they began the long journey back to

what was once the swamp,

but is now the Land of the Free.

Along the way, the Swamp Creatures met a crazy old man.

He looked harmless enough.

But then the crazy old man started beating them with his club.

"OUCH!" they cried, "What do you want?!"

"WHAT DO WE WANT? MONEY!" shouted the crazy old man.

"WHEN DO WE WANT IT? NOW!"

"But...but..."

"NO MONEY—NO PEACE!" shouted the crazy old man.

"We don't have any money," the red dragon said.

"But we know where to get it. Come help us!"

"LEAD ON, COMRADE!" shouted the crazy old man.

Later that day, they met a little girl.

When she saw them, her eyes grew very big.

"The world is going to end!" she screeched.

"If we don't take immediate action,

we'll all be like, EXTINCT!!"

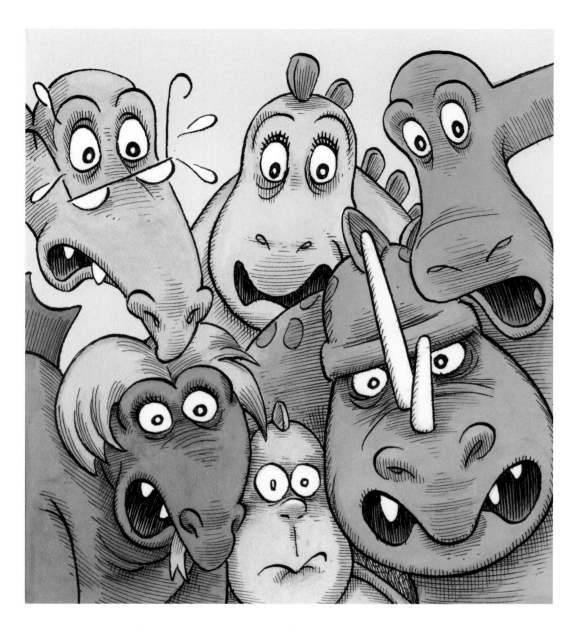

"What can we do?" everyone asked.

"I've got the perfect plan," she said.

"It's called the GREEN RAW DEAL!"

"Raw food is like, healthy, right?" she said.

Raw food was all they knew, but they nodded yes anyway.

"Well the people in the Land of the Free have invented fire!

So now they cook their food!"

"They have no right to eat cooked food!" the little girl said.

"It's unnatural and unhealthy! And besides, fire causes smoke,

which like, hurts your eyes and makes you cough!

We've got to put a TAX on fire and smoke!"

"I can see why it's called the Raw Deal," said the Lobby-o-saurus.

"But why is it called Green?"

"Because it's going to cost them a ton of money!"

the little girl said.

"MOOLAH! The GREEN stuff!"

"You're singing our tune!" said the Swamp Creatures.

"Why don't you join us?"

And so they fell in together and continued their journey.

As they marched along, many other

comrade cavemen joined them.

The Swamp Creatures told them they would take care of them
—once they got to the Land of the Free and took it over.

Meanwhile, Donald and everyone else had

worked hard at building the wall.

Freedom was at stake!

But at last, it was finished.

Donald stood on top of the wall and looked out over the land.

He saw a long caravan headed in their direction.

From so far away, it looked just like a snake!

Donald said they must find out if the approaching crowd

loved freedom or really was like a nasty snake.

"If they don't love freedom,

they'll turn this place back into a swamp real quick!"

When the Swamp Creatures arrived and saw the wall,

they were shocked!

"How dare these people build a wall

around their—I mean around OUR—land?!"

"Walls are mean!" said the little girl.

"Would a pretty flower or happy butterfly build a wall?"

"Who knows!" said the crazy old man.

"Get to the point! My head hurts!"

Then the George-o-saurus spoke, "You can't create

the kind of society we want without breaking a few eggs."

And so, with his loudest voice, he roared,

"NOW HEAR THIS! If you cave people don't let us in,

we'll come in by force!

We are here to take back what is rightfully ours!"

"Dream on, freckle-face!" said Donald.

"You stole this land from these good people,

and turned it into a disgusting swamp.

We are now a free people!

Freedom and Independence forever!"

"But wait," asked the little girl, "doesn't freedom mean NO rules?!

And NO boundaries?"

"Good question," Donald said.

"And the answer is NO!"

So the Swamp Creatures tried to figure out

how to cross the border into the Land of the Free.

But everywhere they looked, there was a wall!

They tried tunneling under it, but it was too deep down.

And they tried climbing over it, but it was just too high!

So eventually, they gave up and went away.

Then one day someone noticed something.

It was a gigantic wooden RINO-saurus on wheels,

just outside the gate.

And it had a tag that said: "For our friends, the cave people!"

"What a nice gesture!" someone said.

"Let's open the door and pull it inside!"

"I'm afraid this could be a trick," said Donald.

"Yes," said one of the Free People.

"A great leader from our past once said, 'trust, but verify!'"

Donald grabbed a torch and approached the RINO-saurus.

He held the fire under the RINO-saurus.

It got VERY hot and started to smoke!

Suddenly a door opened and out jumped the MSNBC–13 gang!

"Don't do it!" they cried. "It was all the Swamp Creatures' idea!!"

And speak of the devil, the Swamp Creatures jumped out next.

And this time, they ran away for good.

After that, if someone wanted to come into the Land of the Free,

that person would knock on the gate,

and someone would check them out.

And if they were freedom-loving, they would be let in.

And if they weren't, they wouldn't. It was that simple.

More and more freedom loving people came

to join the Land of the Free.

And it grew more and more prosperous

and is growing to this day.

BIGLY!

Photo © Josh Del

ERIC METAXAS

ERIC METAXAS has written over thirty children's books, including the bestsellers *Squanto and the Miracle of Thanksgiving* and *It's Time to Sleep, My Love,* illustrated by Nancy Tillman. He has also been a writer for *VeggieTales*.

Since editing the *Yale Record*, the nation's oldest college humor magazine, Eric's humor has appeared in *The New Yorker* and *The Atlantic*. Woody Allen has called these pieces "quite funny." Eric wrote a full-length book parody of the Ripley's "Believe It or Not" books, titled *Don't You Believe It!*, prompting novelist Mark Helprin to call him "the thinking man's Gary Larson (*The Far Side*)."

Metaxas is the bestselling author of *Bonhoeffer: Pastor, Martyr, Prophet, Spy* and many other books, including *Martin Luther, If You Can Keep It, Miracles, Seven Women, Seven Men,* and *Amazing Grace*. His books have been translated into more than twenty-five languages.

He is the host of the *Eric Metaxas Show*, a nationally syndicated radio program heard on more than 300 stations around the US, featuring in-depth interviews with a wide variety of guests.

Metaxas was the keynote speaker at the 2012 National Prayer Breakfast in Washington, D.C., an event attended by the president and first lady, the vice president, members of Congress, and other US and world leaders.

ABC News has called him a "photogenic, witty ambassador for faith in public life," and *The Indianapolis Star* described him as "a Protestant version of William F. Buckley." Metaxas's *Wall Street Journal* op-ed, "Science Increasingly Makes the Case for God" is the most popular and shared piece in the history of the *Journal*.

Metaxas has been featured as a cultural commentator on CNN, MSNBC, and Fox News programs and has been interviewed about his work on the *Today Show, Fox and Friends, The History Channel*, and C-SPAN. He has been featured on many radio programs, including NPR's *Morning Edition* and *Talk of the Nation*, as well as *The Hugh Hewitt Show, The Dennis Prager Show,* and *The Michael Medved Show*.

Metaxas is a Senior Fellow at the King's College in New York City. He lives in Manhattan with his wife and daughter.

TIM RAGLIN

TIM RAGLIN was born and raised in Independence, Kansas, and earned a degree from Washington University's School of Fine Arts in St. Louis. He then immediately launched into the world of freelance illustration, first in St. Louis, then in New York.

Raglin has illustrated many children's picture books, the most popular being *Deputy Dan* and the *Five Funny Frights* series, each having sold over two million copies. He has also worked with Rabbit Ears Productions, a children's video company, and illustrated several of Rudyard Kipling's *Just So Stories*, including the Grammy Award-winning *The Elephant's Child*. Raglin also illustrated and directed his own version of *Pecos Bill*, which won both a Grammy Award for Best Children's Recording and a Parent's Choice Classic Award. Tim served as the creative director of Rabbit Ears until 1991.

He has since illustrated a number of children's picture books, including *The Thirteen Days of Halloween*, *The Wolf Who Cried Boy*, *Twelfth Night*, and *Go Track a Yak!*. But Raglin's chief focus has been his work as the publisher of several of his own picture books, including *Uncle Mugsy* and *The Terrible Twins of Christmas*, which received a Silver Medal from the New York Society of Illustrators. He also published *The Birthday ABC*, which was chosen as an American Library Association "Pick of the List" book in 1995. He is currently working on several new picture books, which he plans to publish under his own imprint, the first of which will be *The Curse of Catunkhamun*.

Raglin has had a number of books chosen to appear in The Original Art Show: The Best in Children's Books, as well as the New York Society's Annual Show. He lives in Independence, Kansas.